Essential English for Hotel and Hospitality Professionals

호텔 & 관광업무 필수 실용 영어

명수진 · 류기환 공저

기문사
KIMOONSA
www.kimoonsa.co.kr

머리말

Preface

이 책은 필수 기초 문법과 쉬운 영어 표현을 사용하여 호텔과 항공 등 환대 산업에서 일하는 근무자들뿐만 아니라 해외를 여행하는 여행객들이 영어로 쉽고 효율적으로 자신을 표현할 수 있도록 하는 것을 목표로 구성했습니다.

각 UNIT별로 호텔 예약, 체크-인, 컨시어지 고객 응대, 프런트 데스크에서 고객 불만 처리하기, 아침식사와 바, 레스토랑, 하우스키핑, 룸서비스, 세탁 서비스, 여러 가지 고객 요청 상황, 체크-아웃, 공항에서의 체크-인, 검색대 및 항공기 내 상황을 분류해 실제 현장에서 일어나는 다양한 기본 상황을 대화로 구성하였습니다. 또한 핵심 표현과 필수 문법은 Essential Phrases로, 미국식 영어 표현과 영국식 영어표현의 차이는 Language tip으로 설명함으로써 영어에 대한 흥미와 함께 실제 대화 상황에서 다양한 표현과 기본 문법을 활용해 조금 더 원활한 대화를 할 수 있도록 했고, 연습문제를 통해 학습한 내용의 이해를 확인할 수 있도록 하였습니다.

이 책을 통해 여행과 업무등 실제적으로 영어 대화가 필요한 다양한 분야에서 일하는 분들이 영어에 대한 과도한 부담을 덜고 쉽고 편하게 영어 표현을 익혀서 효율적이고 원활하게 외국인과 소통하여 더 많은 경험을 쌓을 수 있기를 바랍니다.

저자 일동

차 례

Content

U·N·I·T 01

Reservation

Essential English for Hotel and Hospitality Professionals

UNIT 01

Reservation

Conversation 1 Hotels' reservation

Telephone operator	Good morning. Seoul City Hotel. **How may I help you?**
Caller	OK. **I'd like to make a reservation, please?**
Telephone operator	I'll put you through to reservation. Hold the line, please.
Reservation Staff	Hello. Reservation, Lora speaking. May I help you?
Caller	Yes. I'd like to make a reservation.
Reservation Staff	Certainly, and can I have your name, please?
Caller	My name is James Lesner.
Reservation Staff	OK. All right. so, Mr. James Lesner. **What kind of room would you like?**
Caller	I'd like to reserve a double room.
Reservation Staff	When would you like to stay, sir?
Caller	From the 19th December and for 3 nights.
Reservation Staff	Fine, sir. 19th December and for 3 nights, double room. I'll check availability. Hold on a moment, sir. (after few seconds)

	Yes, we can reserve it for you. Is this a company or individual booking?
Caller	No, I am not from any company. It will be my individual visit.
Reservation Staff	Have you ever been in this hotel before?
Caller	No, I haven't.
Reservation Staff	Would you like one of our Executive rooms, Mr. James Lesner, on the top floor so you can have the stunning see view?
Caller	No, thank you. I can understand it would be great but the thing is I don't like using the lift and also I've got a bad leg. So I was hoping I could have a room near the ground floor.
Reservation Staff	I can understand, sir. No problem at all. I'll make a note of that and I will allocate a room on the first floor for you.
Caller	Thank you. It will be so nice of you.
Reservation Staff	Will you be paying by credit card?
Caller	Yes, the VISA card.
Reservation Staff	And what's the number, please?
Caller	Just a minute. It's 1234 5678 9123 4567.
Reservation Staff	So that's 1234 5678 9123 4567. And your address?
Caller	My address is 10 Harlan street, London, UK.
Reservation Staff	That's fine. I've reserved a room for you. Your reservation number is RS4620. We look forward to seeing you soon.
Caller	Thank you. Goodbye.
Reservation Staff	Goodbye.

Essential Expressions

For room reservation – from customer

- I' d like to book a single room.
- I' d like to book a conference room.
- How much do you charge per night?
- Can I reserve for a double room from 12th to 15th of December?
- Do you have adjoining room?

For room reservation – from Reservation

- What kind of room would you like?
- What will be your period of stay?
- What will be the starting and ending dates of your stay?
- How long do you plan to stay?
- For how many nights do you plan to stay, sir / madam?
- May I please have your name, please?
- Would you please spell the name?
- Are you traveling with the company or is this a personal trip?
- Who is the reservation for?
- Could you give me your address?
- Are you coming by plane?
- When does the flight arrive, sir / madam?
- Can you give me your flight number in case the plane is late?
- When will you be arriving, sir / madam?
- Would you like the hotel limousine to pick you up at the airport?
- We can pick you up at the train station, if you like.

Conversation 2 make a reservation

Staff	Good morning, Metro Hotel.
Caller	Hello, could I speak to somebody in Reservations, please?
Staff	Speaking. How can I help you, sir?
Caller	I want to check availability for later this year. I need two rooms for two nights on December 5th.
Staff	**Let me check,** sir. … **Yes, we still have availability.**
Caller	What's the best rate you can offer?
Staff	**I can offer you** our promotional weekend rate of $119 per room per night, bed and breakfast.
Caller	That sounds great. Please reserve two double rooms for me.
Staff	Of course, sir. Could you give me your name, please?
Caller	It's Leach, Michael Leach.
Staff	Is that L-E-A-C-H?
Caller	Yes, that's right.
Staff	Mr. Leach, **could you give me a credit card number? I need it to guarantee the reservation.**
Caller	Yes. it's Master card and the number is 8192 5212 1327 9964.
Staff	I'll just repeat that : 8192 5212 1327 9964.
Caller	That's correct.
Staff	**Could you tell me the expiry date, please?**
Caller	March 2013.
Staff	Thank you, Mr. Leach. Your reservation number is MH374XY. **We look forward to seeing you in December.** Good bye
Caller	Goodbye.

Essential Phrases

Let me check.
Yes, we [still] have availability.
I can offer you … .
Could you give me a credit card number?

I need it to guarantee the reservation.
Could you tell me the expiry date, please?
We look forward to seeing you in December.

Language Tip

Expiry date

영국 영어에서 '만기 날짜'를 의미한다. 미국에서는 'expiration date'를 사용한다.

Reservation

미국식 영어에서는 '예약'을 의미할 때 항상 'reservation'을 사용한다. 영국식 영어에서는 'booking'도 같은 의미로 함께 사용한다.

Speaking Practice

Staff **[Answer the phone politely.]**
Guest Good morning. I'd like to reserve a single room for January 5th, please.
Staff **[Say you have availability.]**
Guest How much will it cost?
Staff **[Tell the caller your best rate is $140 per night.]**

Guest	Does that include breakfast?
Staff	**[Politely tell caller that it's room only.]**
Guest	OK. I'll take it.
Staff	**[Ask for caller's name and credit card details to confirm the reservation.]**
Guest	It's Gardiner. J Gardiner. My VISA card number is 3412 5624 8742 6908, expiry date 10/14.
Staff	**[Thank the caller and give them the reservation number MH478PT and end conversation politely.]**
Guest	Goodbye.

Conversation 3 Changing Reservation

Sarah	Good morning, Metro Hotel, Sarah speaking.
Caller	Hello, my name is Michael Leach. I'd like to change a reservation, please.
Sarah	Certainly, Mr. Leach. Do you have the reservation number?
Caller	Yes, it's MH374XY.
Sarah	One moment please. Your reservation is for two rooms for two nights, arriving on December 5th.
Caller	Yes, that's correct. Now we need two rooms for three nights.
Sarah	Fine, Mr. Leach. **I've changed that for you.** Your reservation number is the same.
Caller	Thank you.
Sarah	Goodbye.
Caller	Bye.

Conversation 4 Cancelling Reservation

Sarah	Metro Hotel, Good afternoon.
Caller	Hi, I need to cancel my reservation for next Tuesday, March 6th. Can you help me with that?
Sarah	Of course. **Could you tell me your name and the reservation number, please?**
Caller	It's Mrs. Chen and the reservation number is MH374ET.
Sarah	Mrs. Chen, that's fine. I've cancelled your reservation for you.
Caller	That's good.
Sarah	**There's no cancellation charge because you've cancelled within our 48-hour cancellation deadline.**
Caller	Good.
Sarah	**Would you like me to send you a confirmation email?**
Caller	Yes, please. Thank you and goodbye.

Essential Phrases

Could you tell me your name and the reservation number, please?
I've changed that [the reservation] for you.
Would you like me to send you a confirmation email?

I've cancelled your reservation for you.
There's no cancellation charge.
You've cancelled within / outside the cancellation deadline.

Language Tip

Would you like me to … ?

"제가 … 을 해드려도 되겠습니까?"는 표현으로 정중하게 제안할 때 사용한다. 영국식 영어에서는 'Shall I … ?' 를 사용하기도 한다.

[Example]

- *Would you like me to* send you a confirmation email?
- *Shall I* ask someone to carry your bags up to your room?

Speaking Practice

Staff **[Answer the phone politely.]**
Guest Good morning. I need to cancel a reservation, please.
Staff **[Ask for reservation number.]**
Guest The reservation number is MF264FK.
Staff **[Check caller's name and the dates of the stay.]**
Guest Yes, that's correct.
Staff **[Tell caller that's fine and the room is cancelled.]**
Guest Will there be any charge?
Staff **[Tell caller no.]**
Guest That's good. Can you send a confirmation email?
Staff **[Say yes and end call politely.]**
Guest Goodbye.

Language Tip Expressions for Request and Replies

…을 해주시겠습니까?

Could you … please?

- Could you *spell your name*, please?

Would you mind … please?

- Would you mind *giving me your credit card*, please?

부탁을 좀 해도 될까요?

Would you do me a favor?

Could you do me a favor?

Could I ask you a favor?

Could you do a favor for me?

Could you possibly do a favor for me?

Replies [긍정의 대답]

- Of course.
- Sure.
- No problem.
- No trouble at all.
- I'd be glad to.
- It's would be my honor.
- Of course, I will.

Conversation 5 Request

Guest	Excuse me.
Staff	Yes?
Guest	**Could you please do me a favor?**
Staff	**Certainly.** What can I do for you, sir?
Guest	I' m looking for the Sales Department.
Staff	**No problem.** In fact that' s easy. It' s over there, next to the Information Desk.
Guest	Oh, I see. Thanks a lot.
Staff	My pleasure.

Essential Phrases - Introduce with Guests

What' s your name?
Hello, I' m … . / My name is … .
It' s a pleasure / nice to meet you.
I' m glad to meet you.
Nice to meet you, too.

Allow me to introduce myself.
I would like to introduce myself.
I would like to introduce …[my boss, Me. Larson].
Please allow me to introduce …[my friend John].
Let me introduce you to John Smith.
Have we met before?
I don' t think we' ve met before.
You' re new here, aren' t you?

Conversation 6 Introduce 1

Bob Martin	Hello, allow me to introduce myself. My name is Bob Martin. What's your name?
Smith Kar	My name is Smith Kar. I am delighted to meet you Mr. Bob.
Bob Martin	Thank you. Same here.
Smith Kar	Have an enjoyable stay. Hope to meet you soon.
Bob Martin	See you.

Conversation 7 Introduce 2

Staff	Good evening, sir. May I know your name?
Guest	Sure. My name is John Patinson.
Staff	Would you please spell your last name?
Guest	Certainly. P-a-t-i-n-s-o-n, Patinson.
Staff	How do you do, Mr. Patinson? Welcome to our hotel.
Guest	How do you do? Very happy to meet you.
Staff	I wish you'll enjoy your stay in our hotel.
Guest	Yes, I think I will.
Staff	See you later.
Guest	See you.

Conversation 8 Introduce Others 1

Smith	Bob Martin, I would like to introduce Miss Ketty Pearson.
Bob	Hello, Miss Pearson. I am delighted to meet you.
Ketty	Same here, Mr. Bob.

Conversation 9 Introduce Others 2

Karl	Tom, let me introduce my supervisor, Mr. Harries.
Tom	Mr. Harries, I am glad to meet you.
Mr. Harries	Pleasure to meet you, too. Hope to meet you soon.

U·N·I·T

Check-in 02

Essential English for Hotel and Hospitality Professionals

UNIT 02

Check-in

Conversation 1 Check-In

Front Desk Staff	Good afternoon, Madam. How may I help you?
Guest	Good afternoon. I'd like to check-in, please.
Front Desk Staff	Do you have a reservation?
Guest	Yes, I do.
Front Desk Staff	OK. May I have your name, please, madam?
Guest	The name is Hena.
Front Desk Staff	Welcome to City Hotel, Ms. Hena. You have reserved a suite for two nights. Is that correct?
Guest	That's right.
Front Desk Staff	Could you please fill in this registration form?
Guest	Sure.
Front Desk Staff	Thank you. May I have your passport please so that I can fill in your visa number and place of entry?
Guest	Sure.
Front Desk Staff	Thank you. How would you like to pay, madam. By cash or by credit card?

Guest	I'd like to pay with VISA.
Front Desk Staff	Can I make an imprint of your credit card?
Guest	Yes, no problem.
Front Desk Staff	OK. Thank you very much. One last question. What time will you like to check-out?
Guest	I think around eleven o'clock.
Front Desk Staff	Very well. This is your room key. Your room number is 523. Shall I show you to your room?
Guest	Oh, no. thank you. That's not that necessary.
Front Desk Staff	All right. I wish you a pleasant stay with us. The bell boy will take your luggage to your room. And madam, in case you need any help, please don't hesitate to contact us.
Guest	Sure. Thanks for everything.

Conversation 2 Extend Stay

Front Desk Staff	Good morning, sir. What can I do for you?
Guest	I'd like to extend my stay for two nights. Is that possible?
Front Desk Staff	I'll check for you. What is your room number, sir?
Guest	My room number is 454.
Front Desk Staff	Just a moment, sir. Let me check. … Well, Mr. Jonathan, I will be able to extend your reservation for two nights. The only problem is someone has booked your room for those days. I'll try to arrange another room for him so that you don't have to change to another room. As soon as I know the details and arrange everything I'll let you know.
Guest	That would be very nice. Thanks a lot.
Front Desk Staff	You're welcome.

Essential Phrases - Checking In

- I would like to check-in, please.
- Do you have a reservation?
- May I have your name, please?
- Can I make an imprint of your credit card?
- I wish you a pleasant stay with us.
- I hope you will enjoy your stay.
- What can I do for you, madam / sir?
- How would you like to pay, by cash or by credit card?
- I'd like to extend my stay.
- Just a moment, please. I'm going to extend your reservation.
- In case you need any help, please contact us.
- That would be very nice

Language Tip When You Meet Someone

	Greeting	Responses
Formal	• Good morning • Good afternoon • Good evening	• Good morning • Good afternoon • Good evening
Semi formal	• Hello • How are you • How is life	• Hello • Fine, thanks and you? • Nice / Nothing special
Informal	• Hi • so, what' s up • What' s new • Long time no see	• Hi • As always • Nothing • Yeah

Practice - 손님의 대답에 어울리는 인사말 넣기

Staff ________________ , sir?
Guest Good morning.
Staff ________________ , sir?
Guest I' m just fine, young man. What about you?
Staff ______________ , sir. Thank you.

Conversation 3 Check-In with Reservation

Staff	**Good afternoon, Madam. Welcome to the K Hotel.**
Caroline Brown	Good afternoon. My name is Caroline Brown. I have a reservation
Staff	Of course, Ms Brown. One moment, please. Yes, here it is. One double room for three nights.
Caroline Brown	That's correct. Could I have a room on a lower floor, please?
Staff	Is the second floor OK?
Caroline Brown	Yes, that's perfect. Thank you.
Staff	**Could I have your credit card, please?**
Caroline Brown	Yes, here's my VISA card.
Staff	Thank you. You're in Room 209. **Please sign here.** And **would you like a wake-up call?**
Caroline Brown	Oh, yes. Could I have a wake-up call at 7:30 tomorrow, please?
Staff	Of course, 6:30. **Would you like a newspaper?**
Caroline Brown	Yes, I'd like The Korea Times every morning, please. And what time's breakfast?
Staff	**Breakfast is between 7:00 and 10:30**
Caroline Brown	Thank you.
Staff	**Enjoy your stay,** Ms Brown.

Essential Phrases

Good morning/Good afternoon/Good evening.
Welcome to the Metro Hotel.
Could I have your credit card, please?
Please, sign here.

Would you like a <u>wake-up call</u> / <u>newspaper?</u>
Breakfast is between … and … .
Enjoy your stay.

Language Tip

madam vs ma'am

영국식 영어에서 여성 손님을 madam이라 부른다. 미국식 영어에서는 ma'am을 더 많이 사용한다.

lift vs elevator

한국에서 흔히 엘리베이터라 부르는 승강기는 영국에서는 lift, 미국에서는 elevator라는 단어를 사용한다.

'Ms.'

Ms. 라는 호칭은 결혼 여부에 상관 없이 모든 여성에게 붙여 사용할 수 있다.

시간의 표현

- **정각의 경우**

  오전 : (   ) o' clock in the morning = (   ) am
  오후 : (   ) o' clock in the evening = (   ) pm

! 정각이 아닌 경우에는 o' clock을 사용하지 않는다.
10:30 o' clock (X), '10:30' 로 쓰고 ten thirty, half past ten으로 읽는다.

Speaking Practice

Staff	**[Say hello to guest in a friendly way]**
Ms. Yang	Hello, my name is Yang. I have a reservation for one night.
Staff	**[Ask for guest's credit card]**
Ms. Yang	Here's my VISA card.
Staff	**[Ask guest if she wants a wake-up call]**
Ms. Yang	Yes, I would like one at 6 o'clock tomorrow morning, please.
Staff	**[Confirm time and ask guest if she wants a newspaper in the morning]**
Ms. Yang	Yes. Could I have a Wall Street Journal, please?
Staff	**[Say yes]**
Ms. Yang	What time's breakfast?
Staff	**[Tell guest 6:30 to 10:00 and wish a nice stay in the hotel]**

Conversation 4 Check-In with No Reservation

Staff	Good afternoon, sir. **How can I help you?**
Guest	Hi, I need a room for this evening.
Staff	**Do you have a reservation?**
Guest	No, I don't. My flight has been delayed until tomorrow evening and I need to stay in the city overnight.
Staff	**I can offer you our walk-up rate** which is $165 per night for a double room including breakfast.
Guest	That's very expensive. Is that the cheapest rate you have?
Staff	**I'm afraid so. We're very busy this evening.**
Guest	OK. I'll take it.
Staff	Fine. **Could you fill in this guest registration card for me, please?**
Guest	Can I pay by check?
Staff	**I'm afraid not.** Cash or credit card only, I'm afraid. It's hotel policy.
Guest	What time do I have to check out tomorrow?
Staff	Our usual check-out time is 11 o'clock, sir. But with this rate you can have a late check-out until 12 pm.
Guest	That's great, thanks

Essential Phrases

How can I help you?

Do you have a reservation?

I can offer you … .

Our rack rate / walk-up rate is

I' m afraid so. / I' m afraid not.

We' re very busy *this evening* / *this weekend*

Could you fill in this guest registration card for me, please?

Language Tip

Rack rate

Rack rate는 호텔에서 할인이 되지 않은 객실의 가격을 말하며 이 가격을 기준으로 할인율이 정해진다.

Run of the house, walk-up rate라고도 한다.

Post code vs Zip code

우편번호를 뜻하며 post code는 영국에서, zip code는 미국에서 사용한다.

I'm afraid…

'I' m afraid…' 는 부정적인 대답을 해야 할 경우에 예의바르고 부드럽게 표현하기 위해 사용한다.

[Example]

- Can I pay by check? ➡ *I' m afraid* you can' t pay by check.
  / *I' m afraid* ***not***
- Is the restaurant closed? ➡ *I' m afraid* the restaurant is closed.
  / *I' m afraid* ***so***

Practice - I' m afraid so. / I' m afraid not.

1 The hotel doesn' t accept check.
You : ____________________.

2 We have no vacancies this evening.
You : ____________________.

3 You have to check out at noon.
You : ____________________.

4 My room is very small. Can you upgrade it to a suite?
You : ____________________.

5 Do I really have to check out of my room by 12:00?
You : ____________________.

6 Is the bar open now?
You : ____________________.

7 Is that charge for phone calls really correct?
You : ____________________.

Conversation 5 Checking In a Guest Who Has Arrived Early

Staff	Good morning, sir. How are you today?
Guest	Fine, thank you. I have a reservation in the name of Lopez.
Staff	Mr. Diego Lopez?
Guest	Yes, that's right.
Staff	You're staying with us for two nights.
Guest	Yes, that's correct.
Staff	**I'm sorry**, Mr. Lopez. **Your room isn't quite ready yet. Normally our check-in is from** 2 pm.
Guest	Yes, I know that but my flight arrived early.
Staff	**I'm sorry but Housekeeping are still cleaning your room.**
Guest	That's not very good. What do you suggest I do?
Staff	Well, **you're welcome to store** your luggage with us. **May I suggest** you have a cup of coffee in the restaurant? When your room's ready, I'll call and get you. Is that OK?
Guest	OK, but how long will that be?
Staff	**I'll ask Housekeeping to do your room as quickly as possible.**
Guest	Thank you. I'd appreciate it. I want to freshen up and get changed before my meeting. How do I get to the restaurant?
Staff	Just go around the corner to your right, sir.

Essential Phrases - Dealing with Difficult Guests

I' m sorry your room isn' t quite ready yet.
Normally our check–in is from … .
I' m sorry but Housekeeping are still cleaning the room.

You' re welcome to *do / store / wait / sit* … .
May I suggest … ?
I' ll ask Housekeeping to *do / clean / prepare* your room as quickly as possible.

Language Tip

not quite

'The room is ***not quite*** ready yet.' 에서 not quite는 '거의 다 준비된 (almost ready)' 의 의미를 갖는다.

Baggage vs Luggage

Baggage와 Luggage는 거의 비슷한 의미, '짐' , 으로 사용된다. 그러나 Baggage는 주로 일반적인 형태의 가방에 들어 있는 짐의 경우에 사용하는 반면 Luggage는 모든 형태, 예를 들어 종이 박스나 골프백 같은 경우까지 포함된 넓은 범위의 모든 짐에 대해 사용한다.

I' m sorry …

주로 사과할 때 사용하는 표현이지만, 서비스의 경우 나의 실수나 책임이 아닌 경우에도 사용할 수 있다.

Practice - 빈 칸에 적당한 단어 고르기

1 We would be glad to ______ your luggage while you are waiting.
store / sell / lose

2 May I ________ you have a drink in the bar while you are waiting?
suggest / offer / ask

3 I' m sorry, sir. Your room isn' t _________ ready yet.
quite / totally / fully

4 When your room is ready, I' ll come and ________ you.
send / get / check

5 You' re staying with us _________ two night.
for / about / over

6 Our normal check-in time is ________ 2 pm.
from / in / on

7 The coffee shop is just around the corner _________ your right.
to / at / in

Speaking Practice

Staff	**[Greet the guest]**
Mr. Weiler	Good morning. I have a reservation for tonight. My name' s Jens Weiler.
Staff	**[You have been expecting Mr Weiler]**
Mr. Weiler	When can I check in?
Staff	**[Check-in is from 2 pm]**
Mr. Weiler	But I have a very heavy suitcase.
Staff	**[Offer to store his suitcase]**

Mr. Weiler	And what should I do until my room is ready?
Staff	**[suggest a coffee in the coffee shop]**
Mr. Weiler	And where is the coffee shop?
Staff	**[around the corner on the left]**

Language Tip **Asking about Well Being – 안부 묻고 답하기**

	Questions	Answers
• How are you? • How' s life going? • How is your day so far?	In **GOOD** Mood	• Great. • Couldn' t be better. • Fantastic.
• How have you been? • How' s the family? • Did you have a good day?	In **SO-SO** Mood	• Could be worse. • Fair to middling. • I can' t complaint.
• How do you feel? • How was your day? • Have you had a good day?	In **BAD** Mood	• Not too good. • I' ve had better days. • No, it was lousy.

Conversation 6 Asking About Well Being

Guest Service Representative	Good afternoon, welcome in our hotel.
Guest	Hello. I am Mars Karl.
Guest Service Representative	How may I help you, sir?
Guest	I need to check in.
Guest Service Representative	Of course. My name is Sarin Carlston. And I'll be your reservation officer. **How are you today?**
Guest	**I am actually very exhausted** since it was a very long flight.
Guest Service Representative	Well, I will get you checked in as fast as possible so that you can go to your room early and can take rest.
Guest	Thank you so much.

U·N·I·T

03

Looking After Guests – Concierge

Essential English for Hotel and Hospitality Professionals

UNIT 03 Looking After Guests – Concierge

Conversation 1 Concierge 1

Simon	Good evening, madam. **Can I help you?**
Guest	Yes. I've just checked in and I don't have any local currency. Is there an ATM in the hotel?
Simon	Sorry, madam, **I didn't quite catch that.** Is there a what in the hotel?
Guest	An ATM, a cash machine , somewhere I can take out some money?
Simon	Ah, now I understand. I'm sorry, madam, I'm afraid there isn't a cash machine in the hotel but there are lots of banks on Maple Street, which isn't far away.
Guest	Could you show me where it is?
Simon	sure. **Let me give you a map of the city.** The hotel is here. Look, I'll circle it for you. Maple Street **is about five minutes' walk away.**
Guest	Could you show me how to get there?
Simon	Of course. **Turn right out of the hotel. Walk along the street and turn left at the traffic lights.** Walk along Hope Street and then turn right onto Maple Street. There are lots of banks there with cash machines.
Guest	Thank you very much.
Simon	My pleasure, madam.

Essential Phrases

Can I help you?
I didn' t quite catch that.
Let me give you … [a map].

Turn *left* / *right* out of the hotel.
Walk along … .
It' s about … *minutes* / *meters* / *miles* away.

Language Tip

My pleasure

Thank you.' 에 대한 대답이다. 다른 정중한 표현으로는 'You' re welcome.' 이 있다. 좀 더 가벼운 상황에서는 'No problem.' 을 사용할 수 있다.

ATM

Automated Teller Machine' 의 줄임말로 현금 지급기를 의미한다.
동의어 : Cash machine, cashpoint, cash dispenser

I didn' t quite catch that.

잘 듣지 못했거나 이해하지 못했을 때 사용한다. 친근하고 편안한 사이에서 사용하는 표현이다.
정중한 표현으로 'May I beg your pardon?' , 'Pardon me' 등을 사용한다.

Practice - 보기의 단어 중 빈 칸에 알맞은 단어 고르기

catch circle map pleasure turn

1. Sorry, madam. I didn't quite ________ what you said.
2. When you get to the end of the street ________ left into Rothwell Lane.
3. Let me show you where we are on this ________.
4. My ________, madam.
5. I'll ________ the street on this map for you.

Speaking Practice

Staff **[Greet the guest]**
Guest I need to get to the train station. Can you tell me where it is?
Staff **[Give the guest a map ; point to the hotel ; offer to circle it.]**
Guest Thank you very much.
Staff **[Tell the guest the train station is 10 minutes' walk away.]**
Guest OK.
Staff **[Give the guest directions.]**
Guest That's very clear. Thank you very much.
Staff **[Respond politely.]**

Conversation 2 Concierge 2

Simon	Hello, madam. Can I help you?
Guest	Yes. Can you order me a taxi for later today, please?
Simon	Sure, madam, **what time do you need it?**
Guest	I have to be at the Exhibition Center at 10 am.
Simon	OK. **I'll order you a taxi for** a quarter to ten. What's your room number, please?
Guest	Room 1002, Mrs. Hepworth.
Simon	Fine, Mrs. Hepworth. **I'll call your room when your taxi arrives.**
Guest	Thank you very much.
Simon	You're welcome. **Have a nice day.**

Conversation 3 Concierge 3

Simon	Good morning, sir. How can I help you?
Guest	Hello, does the hotel have a business center?
Simon	Yes, but I'm afraid there's a conference in the business center today, sir. But **there are three computers with Internet access in the lobby and all rooms have free Wi-Fi.**
Guest	I need to send a fax abroad.
Simon	Reception will be happy to do that for you. We charge 1 dollar per page.
Guest	OK. And I'm expecting a fax. When it arrives, can you bring it up to my room, please?
Simon	Of course. **We'll do that as soon as it arrives.** Can you tell me your room number, please?
Guest	532. My name is Smith.
Simon	Thank you.

Essential Phrases

What time do you need … ?
I'll order you a taxi for …
I'll call your room when your taxi arrives.
Have a nice day.

There are three computers with Internet access in the lobby.
All rooms have free Wi-Fi.
We'll do that as soon as it arrives.

Language Tip

cab

Taxi를 지칭하는 또 다른 단어이다.

will

손님의 요청에 동의하거나 어떤 것을 하겠다고 약속할 때 사용한다.

[Example]

- *I will* order you a taxi for 9:30.
- *They will* organize it for you.

Practice - 문장 연결하기

1. How can I	A we'll bring it to your room.
2. What time	B when the taxi arrives.
3. As soon as the fax arrives	C help you?
4. I'll order you a taxi	D do you need a taxi?
5. I'll call your room	E for a quarter to ten.

Speaking Practice

Staff **[Greet the guest]**

Guest Yes, I have a question. Does the hotel have a swimming pool?

Staff **[Apologize and tell the guest there is no pool.]**

Guest Oh. What a pity. Never mind.

Staff **[Apologize]**

Speaking Practice

Staff **[Greet the guest]**

Guest Hello. Could you order me a taxi for later, please?

Staff **[Ask the guest what time she needs the taxi.]**

Guest I need it at noon.

Staff **[Tell the guest you will call her room when it arrives.]**

Guest Thank you.

Staff **[Respond politely.]**

U·N·I·T

04

Communication Problems – Front Desk

Essential English for Hotel and Hospitality Professionals

UNIT 04

Communication Problems – Front Desk

Conversation 1 Front Desk 1

Sarah	Good morning, Metro Hotel, Sarah speaking.
Guest	Good morning. This is Rog···.
Sarah	I'm sorry, sir. **It's a very bad line. I didn't quite catch your name. Could you repeat again?**
Guest	This is Rog··· . I want to ··· .
Sarah	I'm sorry, sir. I can't hear you properly. **Could you possibly call back?**
	Guest calls back
Sarah	Good morning, Metro Hotel. Sarah speaking.
Guest	Good morning. This is Roger Dawson. I called a minute ago.
Sarah	Oh, hello, Mr. Dawson. Yes, that's better. How can I help?
Guest	I'd like to speak to Mr. Diamond in Room 721, please.
Sarah	One moment, I'll put you through.

Conversation 2 Front desk 2

Sarah	Good morning, Metro Hotel. Sarah speaking.
Guest	Hello. I'm calling about a reservation I made last week.
Sarah	Do you have the reservation number?
Guest	Yes, it's MH4278JM, no, sorry, I mean JN.
Sarah	I'm sorry. I didn't quite catch the last two letters. **Would you mind repeating the number?**
Guest	It's MH4278JN.
Sarah	Sorry, madam. **Is that M for Mike or N for November?**
Guest	N for November.
Sarah	Thank you. **Let me just read that back to you** : that's MH4278JN. Reservation for Mrs. Harris … .

Essential Phrases

It's very bad line.
I didn't quite catch your name.
Could you repeat that?
Could you possibly call back?

Would you mind repeating … ?
Is that M for Mike or N for November?
Let me (just) read that back to you.

Language Tip

Would you mind + 동사원형 + ing

"… 을 해주시겠습니까?"의 의미로 다른 사람에게 매우 정중하게 부탁할 때 사용하는 표현이다.

[Example]

- *Would you mind spelling* your name?

Practice - 맞는 형태의 동사 고르기

1. Would you mind **to spell / spelling** your name for me?
2. Could you **repeat / repeating** that for me?
3. I'm sorry. I didn't quite **catch / to catch** what you said.
4. could you possibly **calling / call** back?
5. One moment, **I'll put / I put** you through.
6. Let me **reading / read** that back to you.

Speaking Practice

Staff **[Answer the phone politely.]**

Guest Good morning. My name is Mi … . I want to … .

Staff **[Politely tell caller that you can't understand her and ask her to repeat her name.]**

Guest My name is Mi … . I want to ca … .

Staff **[Tell caller you still can't understand her and ask her to call back.]**

Guest Hello. My name is Michelle Williams and I want to cancel a table for dinner.

Staff **[Tell caller that's much better and you will put her through to the restaurant.]**

Guest Thanks.

U·N·I·T 05

At Breakfast and The Bar

Essential English for Hotel and Hospitality Professionals

UNIT 05

At Breakfast and The Bar

Conversation 1 Serving Breakfast

Waiter	Good morning. Could I have your room number, please?
Guest 1	Good morning. We're in Room 406.
Waiter	Thank you. **The continental breakfast is on the buffet** over there. **Feel free to help yourself.** Here are your menus if you'd like something from the kitchen. **I'll come and take your orders in a moment. Can I bring you** some tea or coffee?
Guest 1	Coffee for me, please, with hot milk.
Guest 2	And tea for me.
Waiter	What kind of tea would you like?
Guest 2	English breakfast, please, with milk. And could we have some toast?
Waiter	Of course. Would you like white, brown or wholemeal?
Guest 2	Wholemeal, please.
Waiter	Here's your tea and coffee and your toast. **Would you like anything from the menu?**

Guest 1	I'll have the sausages, scrambled eggs, and hash browns.
Waiter	Madam?
Guest 2	I'd like the blueberry pancakes, please.
Waiter	Thank you. I'll get those for you right away.
	[…]
Waiter	**Here you are. Enjoy your breakfast. Is there anything else I can get you?**
Guest 2	No thanks.

Essential Phrases

Could I have your room number, please?
The continental breakfast is on the buffet.
[Feel free to] help yourself / yourself to the buffet.
Here are your menus.
I'll come and take your orders in a moment.

Can I bring … ?
What kind of *tea* / *bread* would you like?
Would you like anything from the menu?
Here you are.
Enjoy [your breakfast].
Is there anything else I can get you?

Language Tip

Here you are.

"여기 있습니다."의 의미로 손님에게 음식을 드릴 때 사용하는 표현이다.
같은 의미의 표현으로 Here you go / There you go를 사용할 수 있다.

Right away

'일을 신속하게 처리하겠다' 는 의미를 더할 때 때 사용한다.
영국식 영어에서는 straight away, 미국식 영어에서는 coming right up을 같이 의미로 사용한다.

Speaking Practice

Staff **[Say hello to guest politely.]**
Guest Good morning.
Staff **[Ask for room number.]**
Guest I'm staying in Room 872.
Staff **[Continental breakfast or something from the menu?]**
Guest I haven't decided yet.
Staff **[Give guest breakfast menu.]**
Guest Thank you.
Staff **[Ask if she wants tea or coffee.]**
Guest Could I have a pot of Earl Grey tea, please?
Staff **[Milk or lemon?]**
Guest Lemon, please.
Staff **[Offer guest toast.]**
Guest Yes, please. And I don't think I'll have anything from the menu.
Staff **[Invite guest to go to buffet.]**
Guest Thank you.
Staff **[Give guest tea and end conversation politely.]**

Conversation 2 At The Bar 1

Waiter	Good evening, sir. How are you this evening?
Guest	Find, thanks.
Waiter	**What can I get you?**
Guest	I'll have a beer, please.
Waiter	Of course, sir. **Would you like draught or bottled beer?**
Guest	I'd like to try a draught beer. What would you recommend?
Waiter	Well, the German and Czech pilsner on draught are very popular.
Guest	Right. I'll have a Czech pilsner, please.
Waiter	There you are, sir. **That'll be $3.90, please.**

Conversation 3 At the Bar 2

Waiter	Good evening, ladies. What would you like this evening?
Guest	Two gin and tonics, please . And could we have long drinks with lots of ice please?
Waiter	Of course. **Would you like a slice of lemon?**
Guest	Yes, please.
Waiter	Here you are. **Would you like to pay for them now or shall I start a tab for you?**
Guest	I think we'll start a tab. We might have another drink later on.
Waiter	Of course. Could you give me your room number, please?
Guest	I'm in 469.
Waiter	**Could you sign here, please?**
Guest	Thank you.

Essential Phrases

What can I get you?
Would you like draught or bottled beer?
That' ll be [price], please.
Would you like *ice* / *a slice of lemon?*

Would you like to pay for them now?
Shall I start a tab for you.
Could you sign here, please?

Language Tip

On tab

'생맥주' 를 의미한다. 미국식 영어에서는 생맥주를 말할 때 'on draught' 에 비해 'on tab' 을 더욱 보편적으로 사용한다.

달러, 유로로 쓰인 가격을 말할 때

1. 소수점 윗자리 숫자를 말한다.
2. dollar(s), euro(s) 등의 통화를 말한다.
3. 소수점 아래 숫자를 말한다.

[Example]

- $ 7.99 : Seven dollars ninety-nine
- € 6.90 : Six euros ninety

Practice - 자연스러운 대화가 될 수 있도록 문장의 순서 쓰기

____

❶ Would you like ice?
❷ Good evening, sir. How are you this evening?
❸ I' m fine, thank you.
❹ Can you charge it to my room?
❺ Scotch and soda, please.
❻ No, thank you.
❼ It' s 1107.
❽ That' ll be $6.00, please.
❾ What can I get you?
❿ Of course, sir. Can you give me your room number?

Speaking Practice

Staff **[Say hello to guest politely.]**
Guest Good evening, how are you?
Staff **[Answer politely and ask guest what he would like to drink]**
Guest I think I'll have a beer. What bottled beers do you have?
Staff **[Tell guest Grolsch, Heineken and Budweiser]**
Guest What would you recommend?
Staff **[Choose one of the three beers yourself and recommend it.]**
Guest Fine. Then I'll have one of those.
Staff **[Give beer to guest.]**
Guest How much do I owe you?
Staff **[Tell guest 4.00.]**
Guest Can I put it on a tab?

Staff **[Tell guest yes and ask for his room number.]**
Guest I'm saying in Room 406.
Staff **[Thank him and ask guest for signature.]**

Conversation 4 Complaints From Guests At The Bar 1

Waiter	Here's your mineral water with ice and lemon, madam.
Guest	I'm sorry, I can't drink out of that. The glass is dirty and there's lipstick around the edge. Please take it away and bring me another one.
Waiter	**I'm very sorry,** madam. **I'll replace it right away.**
Guest	Thank you.
Waiter	Here you are, madam. I hope this glass is better for you.
Guest	Yes, that looks a lot better, thank you.
Waiter	My pleasure.
Guest	Excuse me?
Waiter	**Is there another problem,** madam?
Guest	I asked for still mineral water, not sparkling.
Waiter	Oh, sorry. **I do apologize.** I'll exchange it at once.

Conversation 5 Complaints From Guests At The Bar 2

Guest	Excuse me. Could we have the bill, please?
Waiter	Of course, sir. That'll be $55.19, please.
Guest	$55? That's very expensive.
Waiter	Well, **that's for your food and two drinks,** sir. And there's a 15% service charge which is added to the bill.
Guest	Service charge?
Waiter	Yes, sir. If you look at the menu, it says a service charge of 15% is added to your bill. **I'm afraid it's hotel policy,** sir.

Essential Phrases

I'm *very* / *really* sorry.

I'll replace it right away.

I hope this one is better for you.

Is there *a* / *another* problem?

I do apologize.

That's for your food and two drinks.

I'm afraid it's hotel policy.

Language Tip

Check / Bill

'계산서'

미국식 영어에서는 'check'을, 영국식 영어에서는 'bill'을 주로 사용한다.

의미를 강조하는 'do'

'사과 드립니다'를 표현할 때 사용하는 'I apologize.'의 의미를 더욱 강하게 표현하고 싶을 때 'do'를 덧붙인다.

I *do* apologize.

Practice - 빈 칸에 들어갈 전치사 고르기

1 Here's your mineral water _______ ice and lemon
by / of / with

2 I'll take it back _______ the bar.
from / to / at

3 Look _______ the menu.
at / by / to

4 The service charge is added _____ the bill.
with / to / by

5 The glass has lipstick _____ it.
on / by / of

U·N·I·T

06

In The Restaurant

Essential English for Hotel and Hospitality Professionals

UNIT 06

In The Restaurant

Conversation 1 Taking a Restaurant Reservation by Phone

Waitress	Good afternoon. The Grill Room Restaurant. How may I help you?
Guest	Yes. Hello. My name is Mike Gordon. I'd like to make a reservation for the evening. There are four of us, and we'd like a table at about 7:00.
Waitress	Yes, Mr. Gordon. We have some very nice window tables for four at 7:00. Would you like smoking or non?
Guest	It's my wife's birthday. Could you put a bouquet of a dozen red roses on the table?
Waitress	Certainly, Mr. Gordon. We'll just add that to your bill. So, we'll see you at 7:00 this evening, Mr. Gordon. The roses will be on the table before you're seated.
Guest	Thank you very much. Bye.

Essential Phrases - Taking a table reservation

- When would you like your table to be reserved?
- A table for how many people?
- Where would you like to seat?
- Is it smoking or non-smoking area?
- May I have your name, please?
- Could you spell your name, please?
- May I have your room number, please?
- May I have your telephone number, please?
- I' m afraid the table is not available at that time. But we can arrange a seat for you at 8:30.
- I' m afraid we' ve fully booked today.
- Would you like me to make a reservation at another restaurant for you?

Conversation 2 Accommodating Guests Who Have No Reservation

Waitress	Good evening, sir. Welcome to City restaurant. Do you have a table reservation?
Guest	No, I' m afraid not.
Waitress	It's okay. Don't worry. Would you like a table in smoking or non-smoking area?
Guest	Non-smoking, please.
Waitress	Please come with me. Is this table alright?
Guest	it' s absolutely perfect.
Waitress	Would you care to take a seat?
Guest	Thanks.

Essential Phrases

Greeting and Seating customer

- Good evening. Do you have a table reservation?
- Would you please come this way?
- Could you please come with me?
- Come with me, please.
- Is this table alright?
- Is this table suitable for you?
- Is this table of you liking?

Conversation 3 Taking an Order

Service Staff	May I take your order, please?
Guest	Not really. I haven't decided.
Service Staff	No problem at all. Take your time. I will come back for taking the order when you will be ready.
Guest	OK. I will call you.
	[After few minutes]
Service Staff	So sir, would you like to order now?
Guest	Yes, first, I'd like to start with a salad?
Service Staff	Certainly. And what kind of dressing would you like?
Guest	French dressing.
Service Staff	What would you like to follow?
Guest	I'd like clam chowder, please.

Service Staff	I must say it is really a good choice, sir. And what's the main course?
Guest	May I have T-bone steak?
Service Staff	Certainly, sir. How would you like your steak?
Guest	Make it medium-rare. And can I have a glass of red wine with my meal.
Service Staff	Yes, of course. And would you care for any dessert? We have a fantastic chocolate cheese cake.
Guest	OK, I'll try a piece with black coffee.
Service Staff	Very good, sir. May I repeat your order?
Guest	Yes, go ahead.
Service Staff	So you would like to have salad with French dressing, followed by clam chowder. Then medium-rare T-bone steak as main course and finally a piece of chocolate cheese cake with black coffee. Is everything all right, sir?
Guest	Yes. Everything is absolutely all right.
Service Staff	Thank you sir. It won't take long.

Essential Phrases - Taking order

- May I recommend our special dish of the day?
- At the moment, we're having a special promotion of German Draft Beer.
- Would you like to order?
- May I take your order, please?
- I will come back for the order when you're ready.
- What would you like to start with?
- And to follow?
- How would you like your steak?
- What kind of dressing would you like with your salad?
- Would you like anything to drink?
- What would you like to drink with your meal?
- This set is enough for 2 persons.
- May I repeat your order? There are … .

Conversation 4 Welcoming Diners, Giving Out Menus, Taking Drinks Orders

Waitress	Good evening, madam. **Welcome to the Metro restaurant. May I take your coats?**
Guest	Good evening. Thanks.
Waitress	**Would you like an aperitif before you order?**
Guest	Yes, please. Could we have two glasses of Prosecco?
Waitress	Certainly. **Let me give you some menus. I'll come back to take your order in a few moments.**
Guest	That's wonderful. Thank you.
Waitress	Of course. We also have some special on the board.
Guest	What are the specials?
Waitress	The specials today are rack of lamb, lemon sole and a vegetarian pasta dish.
	Later
Waitress	Here you are. Two glasses of Prosecco. **Are you having wine this evening?**
Guest	Thank you. Yes, we are.
Waitress	**Here's the wine list.** We have four excellent red and white house wines and on the last pages you'll find the full wine list.
Guest	Thank you.
Waitress	**Let me know when you're ready to order.**

Essential Phrases

Welcome to the [Metro] restaurant.
May I take your coat?
Would you like an aperitif before you order?
Let me give you some menus.
I'll come back to take your order in a few moments.

The specials today are … .
Are you having wine this evening?
Here's the wine list.
Let me know when you're ready to order.

Practice - 예의바르게 말하기

1 Give me your coat.
______________________.

2 Hi. Thanks for coming to eat here!
______________________.

3 here. Take the menu!
______________________.

4 You want wine?
______________________?

5 Tell me when you've decided what you want to eat.
______________________________________.

Conversation 5 Taking Food Orders, Explaining Dishes, Choosing Drinks

Waitress	Good evening, everyone. **Are you ready to order?**
Guest	Not quite. I think we need a little bit longer. Please tell us the specials again.
Waitress	Of course, madam. On the specials board this evening we have lemon sole, rack of lamb and a vegetarian pasta dish.
Guest	It all sounds so nice. I don't know what to have!
Waitress	**Take your time.** I'll be back in a few minutes to take your orders.
	Later
Guest	Excuse me, I think we're ready to order now.
Waitress	Very good, madam. **What are you going to have?**
Guest	No appetizers to start. I'll have the lemon sole and can we have one steak cooked medium rare, please?
Waitress	Excellent choices. **And have you chosen some wine?**
Guest	Yes, we'll have a bottle of the house red, please.
Waitress	Of course, sir. Would you like some water too?
Guest	Yes, a bottle of still, and one sparkling.

Language Tip **코스 메뉴의 구성**

일반적으로 코스 메뉴는 전채 요리, 메인 메뉴, 디저트로 구성된다. 그러나 미국식 영어와 영국식 영어에서 메뉴의 구성과 사용하는 단어에는 차이가 있다.

- 미국식 영어
  Appetizer – main course / entree – dessert
- 영국식 영어
  Starter / appetizer – main course – dessert / sweet / pudding

Practice - 자연스러운 대화가 될 수 있도록 문장의 순서 쓰기

____

❶ Good afternoon, madam. Are you ready to order?
❷ Very good, madam. What are you going to have?
❸ Of course. Still or sparkling?
❹ Not quite. Please give me five more minutes.
❺ I'll have pâté as an appetizer and then a Caesar salad with chicken, please.
❻ Of course. I'll be back in a moment.
❼ No, thank you. But could I have a bottle of water?
❽ Excuse me, I'm ready to order now.
❾ An excellent choice, madam. Are you going to have a glass of wine?
❿ Still please, with ice and lemon.

Conversation 6 Asking About Dessert And Coffee, Bringing The Bill, Handling Payment

Waitress	Sorry to interrupt. **May I clear away your plates?**
Guest	Yes, please do. We've finished.
Waitress	**How were your main courses? Was everything OK?**
Guest	Yes, thank you. It was all excellent.
Waitress	**Would you like to see the dessert menu?**
Guest	No, thank you. I think we'll skip dessert.
Waitress	**Can I bring you anything else?** A coffee or a digestif, perhaps?
Guest	Could we just have two espressos?
Waitress	Of course.
Guest	And then could I have the bill, please?
Waitress	Of course, sir. I'll be back right away with your coffees.
Guest	Can I pay by credit card?
Waitress	Yes, sir. ··· Oh, **I'm afraid we don't accept that kind of credit card,** sir, only VISA and MasterCard.
Guest	OK, then I'll use my VISA card.
Waitress	Here's your bill, sir. **Please put your card in the terminal, enter your PIN, and then press the green OK button.**

Essential Phrases

May I clear your plates?
How were your main courses / was you meal?
Was everything OK?

Would you like to see the dessert menu?
Can I bring you anything else?
We accept … . I' m afraid we don' t accept … .

Practice - 보기의 단어 중 빈 칸에 알맞은 단어를 골라 넣기

afraid use enter press by was accept may

Waiter **1** _______ I clear away the plates?
Guest Of course.
Waiter **2** ____________ everything OK?
Guest Yes, fine, thanks. Can I pay the bill **3** _____ credit card?
Waiter Yes, but I' m **4** __________ we don' t **5** _______ that kind of credit card, madam.
Guest OK. Then I' ll **6** _____ my VISA card.
Waiter Here' s your bill, madam. Please put your car in the terminal, **7** ______ your PIN, and then **8** _______ the green OK button.

Conversation 7 Checking Bill

Guest	May I have my bill, please?
Waiter	certainly, sir. One moment, please. … Here is your bill, sir.
Guest	Thank you. [look at the bill] . Why is this item here?
Waiter	That's vegetable, sir. It was served with your chicken, sir.
Guest	Oh, the vegetables weren't included? I thought it was free.
Waiter	I am sorry but it's not sir. They were extra.
Guest	OK. But wait a moment. See here. You seem to have charged me twice for the dessert. Look here.
Waiter	I'll just go and check if for you, sir. … Yes, sir. You're right. The cashier made a mistake. I am terribly sorry sir. I will come back within few minutes with correct bill.
	few minutes later
Waiter	Here is your new bill, sir. I think you'll find it correct now.
Guest	Thank you. It's OK now.
Waiter	We're very sorry about the mistake.
Guest	Oh, that's all right. Now tell me, can I pay the bill by traveler's check?
Waiter	Certainly, sir. We'll give you the change in local currency, if that's all right.
Guest	Oh. Keep the change.
Waiter	Thank you very much indeed, sir.
Guest	And I'd like a receipt.
Waiter	Certainly, sir. Just moment, please. I will be back very shortly.

U·N·I·T

07

Housekeeping / Room Service / Laundry Service

Essential English for Hotel and Hospitality Professionals

UNIT 07 Housekeeping / Room Service / Laundry Service

Conversation 1 Housekeeping – Dealing With Guests

Maid	Good morning, Housekeeping. Karen speaking.
Guest	Hello. Can you bring us some extra pillows, please?
Maid	Of course, sir. **How many would you like?**
Guest	Could we have four extra ones, please?
Maid	Certainly, sir. **What's your room number?**
Guest	It's Room 406.
Maid	**I'll send them up as soon as I can,** sir.

Conversation 2 Housekeeping – Solving Problems

Maid	Good morning, Housekeeping. Karen speaking.
Guest	Is that Housekeeping?
Maid	Yes, it is. How can I help you?
Guest	We've just come back to Room 369 and our room hasn't been cleaned. The breakfast dishes haven't been taken away and the bed hasn't been made. And we need some fresh towels.
Maid	Oh, I'm very sorry, madam. I'll send a maid right away to clean the room

Essential Phrases

How many [extra …] would you like?
What' s your room number?
I' ll send it / them up as soon as I can.

Sorry to disturb you.
I' ve come to clean your room.
Please hang the sign on the door when you' re ready.

Conversation 3 Housekeeping – Agreeing To Come Back Later

Staff	Good afternoon, Mrs. Ena. Can I clean your room now?
Guest	Could you please come back again. **I' m tied up at the moment.** I' ve some visitors.
Staff	All right, no problem. When would you like me to come back?
Guest	How about 6:00. Is that all right?
Staff	Sorry, Mrs. Ena. **I' ll be off then.** I' ll finish working at 5:30. But please **don' t worry.** One of my colleagues will come.
Guest	OK.
Staff	By the way, did you ask for an adaptor?
Guest	Yes, I need for one.
Staff	I' ve got it for you. Here it is.
Guest	Thank you very much.
Staff	It' s my pleasure.

Essential Phrases

I' m tied up at the moment.	I' ll be off then.
Don' t worry.	I did ask for one.

Language Tip

bring / take

■ **bring**

1. '가져다[제공해] 주다'
2. 어떤 물건을 사람에게 전달 할 경우 사용한다.
3. Example : I' ll bring the towels to your room. [객실에 있는 손님에게 수건을 전달 할 경우]

■ **take**

1. '가지고 가다[이동시키다]'
2. 어떤 물건을 다른 장소로 가져다 줄 경우 사용한다.
3. Example : Take the towels to Room 124. [124호 객실에 수건을 가져다 놓을 경우]

Certainly / Of course

손님이 무엇인가를 요청했을 경우 '해 드리겠습니다' 는 긍정의 대답으로 사용하는 표현.

Practice - bring / take 연습

1. Ali, can you ______ this new bathrobe to Room 21015?
2. Our pillows are too soft. Could you ________ us some firmer ones, please?
3. Where are you going? Karen asked me to _____ these pillows to Room 254.
4. Hello, Mr. Norman. This is Karen from Housekeeping. One of the maids will _________ the new pillows to your room immediately.

Practice - 문장 연결하기

1. I' ve come	A send somebody up immediately.
2. I' ll	B to clean your room.
3. I' m sorry	C I help you?
4. I' ll come	D to disturb you.
5. How many	E back when you' ve finished.
6. How can	F do you need?

Conversation 4 Room Service – Taking Room Service Orders 1

Staff	Room service, can I help you?
Guest	Good morning. Can I order some room service?
Staff	Of course, madam. **What would you like?**
Guest	I'd like a continental breakfast.
Staff	Very good, madam. **Would you like tea or coffee?**
Guest	Coffee. Could I have a cappuccino?
Staff	Certainly, madam.
Guest	How long will that be? I'm in a hurry this morning.
Staff	**It'll be with you in ten minutes.**
Guest	Good.
Staff	**Could I have your room number, please?**
Guest	It's 1002. Mrs. Hepworth.
Staff	Thank you, Mrs. Hepworth. Goodbye.
Guest	Thank you. Goodbye.
	Later
Waitress	Room Service.
Guest	One moment. Just coming!
Waitress	Good morning, madam. Room Service.
Guest	That was quick.
Waitress	One continental breakfast with a cappuccino. **Could you sign here please,** madam? Thank you. **Enjoy your breakfast.**
Guest	Thanks.

Essential Phrases

What would you like?
Would you like tea or coffee?
It'll be with you in [about] … minutes.

Could I have your room number, please?
Could you sign here, please?
Enjoy your breakfast.

Language Tip

Cappuccino

카푸치노. 전통적으로 이탈리아에서 카푸치노는 아침에만 서비스된다.

Continental breakfast

유럽식 아침식사. 일반적으로 커피나 차, 버터와 잼을 곁들인 크라상(croissant)과 과일로 구성된다.

Speaking Practice

Staff **[Answer phone by saying department and your name and asking what the caller wants.]**
Guest Good evening. Is it too late to order some room service?
Staff **[Tell guest it's not too late and ask what guest wants.]**
Guest Could I have a burger with fries and a beer?
Staff **[Reply politely and ask guest what kind of beer.]**
Guest I'll have a Budweiser, please.
Staff **[Ask guest if he wants ketchup with his burger.]**

Guest Yes, please. How long will that be?
Staff **[Tell guest about 15 minutes and end call politely.]**

Conversation 5 Room Service – Taking Room Service Orders 2

Staff	Room service. How may I help you?
Guest	Hello. This is Nancy Parin in room 819. I'd like a Caesar salad, please.
Staff	Certainly ma'am. A large salad or just a side salad?
Guest	A large salad, please. Large enough to be a dinner in itself.
Staff	Right. A large Caesar salad. Would you like anything else, ma'am? Some wine perhaps? Or some other beverage?
Guest	I'll just have some mineral water, please.
Staff	Thank you, ma'am. That will be $12.35 with tax. Your meal should reach you in abcut 30 minutes.

Conversation 6 Room Service – Delivering An Order

Guest	Yes?
Staff	Room service. ··· Does everything look okay?
Guest	I hate to do this to you, but is it too late to order some chicken soup too?
Staff	Not at all, ma'am. We can get that to you in about 10 minutes. That will add about $3.50 to your bill.
Guest	Oh, yes. Thanks.
Staff	Ma'am, would you like to sign this to charge the order to your room? Have a pleasant dinner, ma'am. That soup should be here very soon.
Guest	Well, thanks very much for the great guest service. This is for you.

Conversation 7 Laundry Service 1

Laundry Staff	Good afternoon. Laundry Service. May I help you?
Guest	Good afternoon. This is Andrew speaking. I just checked-in and I'll have a meeting in a few hours, but my suite is folded. Can I have it pressed within few hours?
Laundry Staff	That is no problem, sir. So, you need it within a few hours?
Guest	Well, I'll rather have it within an hour. It's very urgent.
Laundry Staff	OK. But there is a surcharge for express service.
Guest	I know. But that is fine with me. I need it to be pressed as early as possible.
Laundry Staff	All right. I will send someone to pick it up in a few minutes.
Guest	But listen I won't be in my room then because I have to leave straight away. I'll put my suite on the bed. Is it OK?
Laundry Staff	No problem. What is your room number, sir?
Guest	My room number is 208.

Conversation 8 Landry Service 2

Guest	Hello.
Laundry Staff	Good morning, Mr. Piter. this is the laundry office. You asked us to try to remove the stain in your shirt.
Guest	Yes. That is right. Did it work?
Laundry Staff	Well, we've tried but it is not so easy. So far it didn't work very well. We can try another time, but then the colors might fade.
Guest	Oh, no, I was afraid this might happen.
Laundry Staff	What shall we do, Mr. Piter?
Guest	What if you remove the stain and the color will fade? Can you dye the shirt for me?
Laundry Staff	No, I'm sorry. I am afraid that wouldn't be possible.
Guest	Well, then I feel I have no other option left. I think the best is just to wash the shirt and leave the stain as it is.
Laundry Staff	OK. We will try our level best. There is another thing I want to inform you. There is a hole in your shirt at the back. I believe you may aware of it.
Guest	Really? Is there? Sorry. I didn't know.
Laundry Staff	Yes, but it isn't bad. It's a line of stitching that goes loose. We can fix it for you.
Guest	Really? That would be very nice.
Laundry Staff	All right. We will wash your shirt and repair the hole. Wish you a nice day, sir.
Guest	Thank you very much and thanks for calling.

Essential Phrases - Laundry Service

- My suit is folded. Can I have it pressed?
- There is a surcharge for express service.
- I' ll send someone to pick it up.
- Don' t use any detergent of soap.
- Do not tumble dry.
- My shirt is badly shrunk.
- Can you stretch them?
- We are not able to remove the stain.
- Can you dye the blouse for me?
- There is a hole in your trousers.

U·N·I·T

08

Guest Services

Essential English for Hotel and Hospitality Professionals

UNIT 08 Guest Services

Conversation 1 Ordering Things For Guests

Staff	Good morning, sir. **What can I do for you?**
Guest	Hello. I'd like to order some flowers. It's my wife's birthday tomorrow.
Staff	Of course, sir. What kind of flowers would you like?
Guest	A bouquet of red roses, please. Could you have them delivered tomorrow morning at 9:30?
Staff	Certainly, sir. **I'll take care of that for you.**

Conversation 2 Making Appointments

Staff	Hello, madam. **How can I help you?**
Guest	Is there a hairdresser in the hotel?
Staff	I'm afraid not, madam. But **I can make you an appointment** at a local salon **if you like.**
Guest	Yes, please. Could you do that for me? I'd like an appointment at 11:30. Mrs. Lee.
Staff	Of course, Mrs. Lee. **I'll call them now.**

Conversation 3 Checking Information

Guest	Hi, would you look something up for me?
Staff	Yes, certainly, madam. **What would you like me to look up for you?**
Guest	Could you check which terminal my flight leaves from? The flight number is EM693 to Dubai.
Staff	One moment. **I'll just check for you.** It leaves from Terminal 3, at 13:50.
Guest	Thanks very much.

Essential Phrases

What can I do for you?
I'll take care of that for you.
How can I help you?
I can make an appointment if you like.

I'll call them now.
Would you like me to look something up for you?
I'll just check for you.

Language Tip

look up [something] / *look* [something] *up*

인터넷 등을 통해 정보를 확인해 볼 때 사용하는 표현이다.

[Example]

- I'll *look up* the flight times for you.

at + 시간, on + 요일, in + 월

[Example]

at 9:30 / on Monday / in October

- '주말에'를 뜻하는 표현으로 미국식 영어에서는 'on the weekend'를, 영국식 영어에서는 'at the weekend'를 사용한다.

Practice - 문장에 알맞은 전치사 골라 넣기

for of up at on in

1. Can you look something ____ for me?
2. I'll check the flight time ______ the internet.
3. The flight leaves ______ 7:30.
4. What can I do _____ you?
5. The swimming pool opens ____ June.
6. I'll take care ___ that for you.
7. No, thank you. But could I have a bottle __ water?

Conversation 4 Tell About Business Center

Guest	I need to check my e-mail. Is there an Internet cafe near here?
Staff	Certainly, sir. The Business Center at the hotel has Internet access.
Guest	Can I also surf the internet there? I need to find some information for a meeting.
Staff	Absolutely, sir.
Guest	Can I also save information to a disk or pen drive?
Staff	Of course.
Guest	Do you know how much it costs?
Staff	For using the business center for 30 minutes we charge $20.
Guest	OK, thank you.
Staff	My pleasure, sir.

Conversation 5 Asking For Hotel's Facilities Over Telephone

Front Desk Agent	Good morning, City Hotel. May I help you?
Caller	Good morning. I would like to reserve a room but can you tell me a little about the hotel?
Front Desk Agent	I'd be glad to, sir. Our hotel is a resort and spa hotel right beside the beach of Treasure Island. There are Thai and European restaurant, coffee shop and bars. We have sauna, fitness, swimming pool and water sport facility. We also have scuba diving facility for the guests as well as the private boat for the diving trip. What else should I tell you … the price of standard room is $85 per night, a deluxe is $125 and a suite is $185.
Caller	How can I get to the hotel?
Front Desk Agent	We provide the delivery from airport to the hotel.
Caller	That sounds interesting. I will think about it and call you back.
Front Desk Agent	Thank you for calling, sir. You can visit our website at www.cityhotel.com. You can also make an online reservation through it, sir.
Caller	Thank you so much. goodbye.

Essential Phrases

Tell guests about the hotel facilities

- There is a large swimming pool in our hotel.
- There are many places you should visit around here.
- The hotel has the splendid decoration.
- We offer our guest the best sea view in this area.
- We have the health spa for guests to relax and to rise up their good health.

Expression for enquiry

- Can you tell me a little about the hotel?
- Can I have some information about hotel' s facilities?
- May I have some information about the hotel?
- What facilities do you have in the hotel?
- Which restaurant in the hotel has a French menu?
- Do you know where I can find fine jewelry?
- Where' s a good place to see a movie?
- I am looking for a good restaurant. Do you know of any?

Conversation 6 Recommendation For Places To Eat - Making Restaurant Recommendation

Guest	Good evening, Simon.
Staff	Good evening, Mr & Mrs Hepworth. Have you had a good day?
Guest	Yes, thanks. Simon, can you recommend a good Indian restaurant?
Staff	Well, the most famous one in the city is the Majestic on Bristol Street but **it gets very busy.** On Friday nights **you usually have to make reservations.**
Guest	I see.
Staff	But, in fact, **I think the Taj Mahal is better than the Majestic.** Also, it's cheaper. And **it's closer,** too. **I'd recommend that.**
Guest	Sounds good. Could you make reservation for us?
Staff	**You don't usually need reservations.**
Guest	OK, can you show us where it is on a map?
Staff	Of course.
	Later hat evening
Staff	Hello, again. **How was your meal?**
Guest	Simon, thanks very much for your tip. It was an excellent recommendation. The food was great and the service was wonderful. And it was so cheap.
Staff	**I'm glad you liked it.**

Essential Phrases

It gets very busy.

You usually have to make reservations.

You don't usually need reservations.

I think restaurant X is better / cheaper than Y.

It's closer.

I'd recommend that.

How was your *meal* / *evening*?

I'm glad you liked it.

Language Tip

I'd recommend … .

'… 을 추천하고 싶습니다.'는 표현으로 어떤 것을 권하거나 조언을 할 때 사용하는 표현이다.

[Example]

- *I'd recommend* the Taj Mahal.
- *I'd recommend* going to / eating at the Taj Mahal.

I think … .

'제 생각에는 …' 의 의미로 어떤 것에 대한 자신의 생각을 이야기할 때 사용하는 표현이다.

[Example]

- *I think* the Taj Mahal is better than the Majestic.

Practice - 비교급 만들기

1. The Majestic is __________ than Bella Roma. [big]
2. Le Pont Bistro is _________ than the Majestic. [cheap]
3. Bella Roma is __________ than Le Pont Bistro. [expensive]
4. The Majestic is _________ than Le Pont Bistro. [popular]
5. Le Pont Bistro is ____________ than Bella Roma. [small]
6. Bella Roma is _________ than the Majestic. [close]

U·N·I·T

09

Check-Out

Essential English for Hotel and Hospitality Professionals

UNIT 09

Check-Out

Conversation 1 Farewell To Guests

Staff	Good morning, Mr. Stewart. How are you today?
Guest	Good morning. I'm fine, thanks, and you?
Staff	I'm fine, too. Are you checking-out today?
Guest	Yes, I think so.
Staff	Did you enjoy your stay here?
Guest	Yes, I did.
Staff	I hope our service has been up to the mark and you are satisfied.
Guest	sure. I'm delighted with everything here.
Staff	Thank you. I am wishing you to have a nice trip and looking forward to seeing you again.
Guest	Thank you. I'll definitely come here again.

Essential Phrases - Farewell to Guests

More Formal

- Good bye.
- Thank you for coming. Have a nice day.
- Goodbye, please come again.
- Goodbye, I hope to see you again.
- Have a good weekend.
- Have a safe trip.
- Look forward to seeing you again.
- Thank you for coming. / Thanks for coming.
- It was nice to see you.

Less Formal

- See you later.
- I have to run. / I have to go now.
- Catch you later.
- See you again.
- Good bye for now.

Conversation 2 Checking Guests Out, Checking Items On The Bill, Saying Goodbye 1

Guest	Good morning. I'd like to check out, please.
Staff	Good morning, sir. What was your room number?
Guest	Room 532.
Staff	532 ··· Mr. Smith. **How was your stay,** Mr. Smith?
Guest	It was great, thank you.
Staff	**Are you using the same credit card you gave me when you checked in?**
Guest	Yes, that's right.
Staff	Fine, Mr. Smith. Please have a look at this printout : two nights' accommodation, breakfast on Saturday and Sunday morning, bar drinks from Friday and last night, three phone calls and two newspapers.
Guest	Yes, that's correct.
Staff	**Did you have anything from the minibar last night?**
Guest	Oh, yes. I almost forgot. We had two bottles of mineral water last night.
Staff	OK. **I'll add those to your bill. Could you sign here, please?** Thank you. Would you like me to staple your credit card slip to your bill?
Guest	Yes, please. And here are our key cards.
Staff	Thank you. There you are, Mr. Smith. **See you next time. Have a safe trip home. Goodbye.**

Essential Phrases

How was your stay?

Are you using the same credit card [you gave me when you checked in]?

Please have a look at this printout.

Did you have anything from the minibar?

I'll add *that* / *those* to your bill.

Could you sign here, please?

See you next time.

Have a safe trip home.

Practice - 주어진 단어를 이용해 문장 만들기

1 please / here / you / sign / could

____?

2 stay / was / how / your

____________________________?

3 have / the / you / anything / minibar / did / from

_______________________________________?

4 home / safe / trip / have / a

___________________________.

5 the / card / same / you / are / credit / using

___________________________________?

Speaking Practice

Guest	Hello. I'd like to check out, please.
Staff	**[Respond to request and ask for room number.]**
Guest	Room 631.
Staff	**[Give guest printout and ask him to check the bill.]**
Guest	That looks all correct.
Staff	**[Ask guest for credit card.]**
Guest	Here you are.
Staff	**[ask guest for signature.]**
Guest	Of course. Could you staple my credit card slip to the bill, please?
Staff	**[Agree and give papers to guest.]**
Guest	Thank you.
Staff	**[Respond to guest's thanks and ask if everything was OK.]**
Guest	Yes, it was a great weekend. I'm sure we'll be back.
Staff	**[Wish guest safe trip and end conversation politely.]**

Conversation 3 Checking Guests Out, Checking Items On The Bill, Saying Goodbye 2

Guest	Good morning. I'd like to check out, please.
Guest Service Staff	Good morning. May I have your room number, please?
Guest	My room number is 523.
Guest Service Staff	OK. Mrs. Walton. Did you use anything from the mini bar last night?
Guest	Yes, I did. I took a mango juice.
Guest Service Staff	All right. Here is your bill. This is the total amount. Would you please check as if there is any mistake or not?
Guest	OK. I have found everything absolutely all right.
Guest Service Staff	Thanks, madam. Now could you please sign your bill and your credit card imprint? (after signing) All right, madam. Thank you very much. (puts the bill an envelope and gives it to the guest) Here you are, Mrs. Walton. Thank you for staying with us and we hope to see you very soon. Take care.
Guest	Thanks a lot. Bye bye.

Essential Phrases - Checking out

- May I have your room number?
- Did you use something from the mini bar last night?
- Here is your bill.
- This is the total amount.
- Would you please check if there are any mistakes?
- Could you please sign your bill and credit card slip?
- Thank you for staying with us.
- We hope to see you soon.

Conversation 4 Correcting Mistakes On The Bill

Guest	Excuse me, but this bill isn't correct. There are some incorrect charges on it.
Staff	**What's the problem, sir?**
Guest	There are nine phone call charges but I never used the phone in my room. I used my own mobile phone!
Staff	I'm sorry, sir. I don't know how that happened! **I'll remove those and adjust your bill.**
Guest	OK. Thank you.
Staff	I do apologize, sir. **Is everything else OK?**
Guest	Yes. Everything else is fine. Thank you.

Conversation 5 Keeping Guests Happy

Staff	There you are, madam. Here's your credit card and your bill. **How was your stay?**
Guest	Actually, not very good. It was very noisy last night and I couldn't sleep.
Staff	Oh, **I'm sorry to hear that,** madam. What caused the noise?
Guest	There are a noisy group staying on my floor. They came back very late and woke me up.
Staff	Oh, my apologies. **I'll put a note in your file** and make sure you get a quieter room next time. **I'll also pass your comments on to our General Manager.**
Guest	OK. thank you. I know it wasn't your fault.
Staff	**I'm sure it won't happen next time you stay with us,** madam.

Essential Phrases

What's the problem, <u>sir</u> / <u>madam?</u>

I'll remove the charges.

I'll adjust your bill.

Is everything else ok?

I'm sorry to hear that.

I'll put a note in your file.

How was your stay?

I'll pass your comments on to our General Manager.

I'm sure it won't happen next time you stay with us.

Language Tip

look forward to + [동사-ing]

'[동사-ing]를 기대하고 있겠습니다.' 는 의미의 영어 표현이다. look forward to 다음에는 반드시 [동사 원형 + ing]를 사용한다.

[Example]

- I *look forward to* see*ing* you again.

Practice - 보기의 단어 중 빈 칸에 들어갈 알맞은 단어 고르기

adjust happen hear put pass remove

1. I'll ________ the incorrect call charges.
2. I'll ________ on your comments to the hotel manager.
3. I'm sure it won't ________ again, sir.
4. I'll ________ a note in you guest file.
5. I'm sorry to ________ that, madam.
6. I'll ________ your bill, sir.

Practice - 주어진 문장을 'look forward to 동사-ing'를 사용하여 정중한 표현으로 바꾸기

1 See you again soon.
_______________________________________.

2 Welcome you back to the Metro Hotel.
_______________________________________.

3 Show you our new gym and swimming pool.
_______________________________________.

4 Hear your thoughts on the new hotel design.
_______________________________________.

5 Read your comments in our visitors book.
_______________________________________.

U·N·I·T

10

At The Airport

Essential

English

for

Hotel

and

Hospitality

Professionals

UNIT 10

At The Airport

Conversation 1 Check-In 1

Staff	Good morning, sir. Can I see your ticket and passport?
Passenger	Certainly. There you are.
Staff	Thank you. Okay. How many suitcases will you be checking in?
Passenger	Just one suitcase.
Staff	Did you pack your bags yourself?
Passenger	Yes, I did.
Staff	Do you have any electrical goods?
Passenger	I have an electric shaver in my hand luggage. Is that OK?
Staff	that's fine. So nothing in your suitcase?
Passenger	Yes.
Staff	Would you like a window or aisle seat?
Passenger	A window seat, please.
Staff	OK. Just one moment, please. Here's your boarding pass. This is your seat number and the departure

	gate. You can go straight through to the departure lounge. Enjoy your flight.
Passenger	What time will I be boarding?
Staff	We begins boarding at 7:00.
Passenger	Thank you.

Essential Phrases

Ask guests to wait

- One moment, please.
- Just one moment, please.
- Please excuse me a moment.
- Would you excuse me for one moment, please?
- Would you mind waiting a moment, please?
- If you would excuse me for a moment, I' ll find out for you.

Deal with a guest who has been kept waiting

- I' m sorry to keep you waiting, sir / madam.
- I' m sorry to have kept you waiting, sir / madam.
- Thank you for your patience, madam / sir.

Conversation 2 Check-In 2

Staff	Good afternoon. Where are you flying today?
Passenger	Los Angeles.
Staff	May I have your ticket, please?
Passenger	Here you go.
Staff	Are you checking any bags?
Passenger	Just one.
Staff	Okay. Please place your bag on the scale.
Passenger	Well, I have a stopover in Chicago. Do I need to pick up my luggage there?
Staff	No, it'll go straight to Los Angeles. Here's your boarding pass. Your flight leaves Gate 15 and it'll begin boarding at 3:20. Your seat number is 26E.
Passenger	thanks.

Conversation 3 Check-In 3

Passenger	Good morning. How may I help you?
Passenger	The machine didn't recognize my passport.
Staff	I can help. **Where are you flying to today?**
Passenger	Rio. We're flying to Rio and then we have a connecting flight to Recife.
Staff	**Are you checking any bags?**
Passenger	Yes, just one.
Staff	**Can you put it on the scale?**
Passenger	Sure, can you check our bag through the Recife?
Staff	No, I can't. You need to pick it up in Rio to go through customs.
Passenger	How much time do we have? How long is our layover?
Staff	About two and a half hour.
Passenger	that's plenty of time.
Staff	Here are your boarding passes.
Passenger	Thank you.
Staff	**Your flight leaves from Gate 19 and boarding begins at 11:20.** Have a great trip.
Passenger	We will.

Key Phrases

Where are you flying to today?
Are you checking any bags?

Can you put it on the scale?
Your flight leaves from Gate ___ and boarding begins at _______ .

Conversation 4 Check-In 4

Passenger	Hello.
Staff	Good morning. **Where are you flying to** today?
Passenger	I'm going to London.
Staff	And **have you checked in online already?**
Passenger	Yes, I have. But I was wondering, can I change my seat? I have an aisle seat, but I'd really like a window seat if that's possible.
Staff	Let's have a look. **Can I have your passport, please?**
Passenger	Yes, of course.
Staff	Thank you. One minute, **let me check whether there's another window seat available.** Yes, we can do that, sir.
Passenger	Excellent.
Staff	Do you need a paper copy of your boarding pass?
Passenger	No, thanks. I have it on my phone.
Staff	And **do you have any bags to check in?**
Passenger	No, I only have a carry-on bag.
Staff	That's fine. You just need to put this tag on it.
Passenger	Like this?
Staff	That's perfect. Well, you're ready to go. **Enjoy your trip.**
Passenger	Thank you very much.

Key Phrases

Have you checked in online already?
Can I have your passport, please?
Let me check whether there's another window seat available.

Do you have any bags to check in?
Enjoy your trip.
See you next time.

Conversation 5 Check-In Problems

	Baggage is overweight
Staff	I'm sorry ma'am. But **your bag is overweight.** The limit is 23 kilos. **You either need to take some things out or pay for the excess.**
Passenger	How much is the excess?
Staff	It's fifty euros for a bag up to 32 kilos.
Passenger	that's expensive. I'll try to take some things out.
	Flight is delayed
Staff	I'm sorry, but the flight is delayed by at least two hours.
Passenger	So, when do you expect the plane to leave?
Staff	Right now, we expect it to depart at 10:30 p.m. **I do apologize for the inconvenience.**
Passenger	Well, I guess there's nothing we can do.

Staff	**Thank you for your patience.** You can check the departure boards for updated boarding times and flight information.
	Flight is cancelled
Staff	I' m sorry, but **your flight has been cancelled due to** bad weather.
Passenger	But I really need to be in London tomorrow afternoon. What' s the next available flight?
Staff	**Let me see what we can do.** We do have a flight leaving tomorrow morning that I can switch you to.
Passenger	What time in the morning?
Staff	It leave here at 7 a.m. and arrives at 10:00.
Passenger	That will be fine.
Staff	Right, here' s a printed confirmation. And again, I am very sorry for the trouble.
Passenger	That's okay. It's not your fault. Are there any hotel near the airport?
Staff	Yes, of course. **If you go to the customer service desk,** just over there, **you can claim a voucher for a hotel and meals.**
Passenger	Excellent, thank you.
Staff	You' re welcome.

Essential Phrases

Your bag is overweight.

You either need to take some things out or pay for the excess.

I do apologize for the inconvenience.

Thank you for your patience.

Your flight has been cancelled due to … .

Let me see what we can do.

If you go to the customer service desk, you can claim a voucher for a hotel and meals.

Language Tip

감사의 표현

- Thanks.
- Thank you.
- Thank you very much.
- Thank you so much.
- Many thanks.
- Thank you for your kindness.
- Thank you for your trouble.
- You are so kind.
- It's my pleasure to serve you.
- I appreciate your kindness.
- I'm very grateful to you.
- That's very kind of you.

감사에 대한 대답

- You're welcome.
- You are most welcome.
- You're quite welcome.
- My pleasure.
- It's my pleasure.
- Don't mention it.
- It was really nothing.
- Not at all.
- No problem.
- Thank you, sir / ma'am. I'm glad you like it.

Conversation 6 Security Check 1

Security officer	Please lay your bags flat on the conveyor belt, and put your mobile phone and all electronic devices in the bin.
Passenger	Do I need to take my laptop out of the bag?
Security officer	Yes, you do. Please take off your jacket, too.
Passenger	No problem. No I don't think so.
Security officer	Please step back. Do you have anything in your pockets? Keys, cell phone, loose change?
Passenger	I don't think so. Let me try taking off my belt.
Security officer	OK. Come on through.
Passenger	Thank you.

Conversation 7 Security Check 2

Security officer	Is this your bag, sir?
Passenger	Yes, it is.
Security officer	We need to search it. **Do you have any liquids over 100ml?**
Passenger	No problem. No, I don't think so.
Security officer	I'm afraid we need to take this bottle. You're allowed containers up to 100 ml maximum.
Passenger	Okay, I'm sorry. I completely forgot.
Security officer	And this Swiss Knife has to go, too.
Passenger	But, it's important to me!
Security officer	I can take it or **you'll have to go back and check this bag.**
Passenger	Well, I don't have time for that. I guess you'll have to take it.
Security officer	Very well, sir. Here's your bag.
Passenger	Thanks.

Conversation 8 Security Check 3

Passenger	Excuse me. I'm really late for my flight. Can I go to the front of the line?
Security officer	Okay, come forward quickly. Make sure everything is out of your pockets and **please place laptops in a separate tray.** Please step over this way, ma'am.
Passenger	I'm really late for my flight. Could I just …
Security officer	Ma'am, please step over here. **Stand on the marks on the floor and raise your arms above you. Do you have anything in your pockets?**
Passenger	Yes, sorry. I still have some money and my keys.
Security officer	**Please put them in the tray and come through again.**
Passenger	And where's my bag?
Security officer	It looks like your bag needs to be searched.
Passenger	This is ridiculous. I'm going to miss my flight.
Security officer	Do you have anything sharp in here?
Passenger	No, nothing.
Security officer	You can't take the jars on the airplane.
Passenger	Why not?
Security officer	It's a liquid, ma'am. No liquids over 100ml.
Passenger	This is crazy! It's only honey.
Security officer	**I'm afraid those are the rules.**
Passenger	Fine. Keep them.

Essential Phrases

Do you have any liquids over 100 ml?
You' ll have to go back and check this bag.
Stand on the marks on the floor and raise your arms above you.
Please place laptops in a separate tray.
Do you have anything in your pockets?
Please put them in the tray and come through again.
It looks like your bag needs to be searched.

Conversation 9 Immigration 1

Immigration Officer	Good afternoon. May I see your passport, please?
Passenger	Yes, here it is. And here's my visa.
Immigration Officer	Thank you. You have a tourist visa for three months.
Passenger	Yes, that's right. I plan to travel some in the USA.
Immigration Officer	Where are you going?
Passenger	I'm going to spend some time in Atlanta. After that I'm going to Washington, Chicago and California.
Immigration Officer	All right. Enjoy your stay.

Conversation 10 Immigration 2

Passenger	Hello.
Immigration Officer	Good afternoon. What is the purpose of your visit?
Passenger	I have a business meeting.
Immigration Officer	Where is the meeting to be held?
Passenger	It's at a law firm in London.
Immigration Officer	And how long will you be staying?
Passenger	Until Tuesday.
Immigration Officer	Please put your right hand on the scanner. Thank you. Now look at the camera here. 1, 2, 3 ··· . That's great. Thank you and enjoy your stay.
Passenger	Thank you.

Conversation 11 Customs

Officer	Good afternoon. Anything to declare?
Passenger	Excuse me? I don't understand.
Officer	Do you have any valuables or alcohol to declare?
Passenger	No, nothing at all.
Officer	OK. You can go ahead.
Passenger	Thank you.

Essential Phrases

What is your final destination?
How long will you be staying in … ?
What is the purpose of your visit?

How much currency are you carrying (with you)?
Who packed your bags?
Do you have anything to declare?

U·N·I·T

11

In The Cabin

Essential

English

for

Hotel

and

Hospitality

Professionals

UNIT 11 In The Cabin

Conversation 1 Boarding 1

Flight attendant	Good morning, madam. Welcome on board.
Passenger	Thanks.
Flight attendant	Can I see your boarding pass, please?
Passenger	Yes, ··· here you are.
Flight attendant	27G ··· go straight across to the other side, and then turn right. You'll see the seat numbers on the overhead lockers. My colleague will show you where your seat is.
Passenger	Thank you.
Flight attendant	Hello, madam. Welcome on board ··· you're together? Turn right here, go straight down the cabin past the toilets. You'll find your seats at the front of the next cabin, in the middle section. ··· Hello, how are you today, sir? May I check your boarding pass ···

Conversation 2 Boarding 2

Flight attendant	Can I help you, madam? Seat number 17D. Yes, come this way. Yours is the aisle seat just here.
Passenger	An aisle seat? I specifically asked for a window seat.
Flight attendant	Did you? I am sorry. You've been given an aisle seat. Did you request a window seat at check-in?
Passenger	Yes, ··· and I told her I can't fly if I can't have a seat by the window. She assured me I had a window seat.
Flight attendant	Oh, I'm really sorry about this. But don't worry. The flight isn't full today and I'm sure I can sort out a window seat for you. Would you mind just taking this seat until I have checked the passenger list? It will only take a couple of minutes.
Passenger	Are you sure? I don't want to stay here for the flight.
Flight attendant	Don't worry. I'll be back in a moment with a better seat for you, madam.

Essential Phrases - Formal Apologies(정중하게 사과하기)

Expressions

- Excuse me.
- I'm *so* / *very* / *terribly* sorry.
- I do apologize for [my mistake].
- I didn't mean for that to happen.
- Please forgive me for [my mistake / coming late].
- It's all my faults. I'm very sorry.
- Please accept our apology.
- I assure you it won't happen again.

Answers

- That's all right.
- Never mind.
- Not at all.
- No problem.

Practice - 빈 칸에 정중하게 사과하는 표현 넣기

Guest Excuse me. I think there is a mistake in my bill.

Staff ____________ to hear that. I'll check for you right away. Would you please wait a moment?

Guest OK. [a moment later]

Staff _________. There is a mistake in your bill. __________ __________.

Guest Well. ______________ . Please be very careful next time.

Staff Sure, sir.

Conversation 3 Boarding 3

Flight attendant	Excuse me, sir. Would it be alright if we put your bag in the overhead bin?
Passenger	Em, well … . I'd prefer to keep it with me.
Flight attendant	It's just that you're sitting in an emergency exit row. We can't have anything on the floor.
Passenger	OK, do what you must.
Flight attendant	I also need to ask you to raise your window blind and make sure your seat back is in the upright position for take-off.
Passenger	Why do I have to do all this?
Flight attendant	It's standard procedure for take-off, sir. You can recline your seat and take your bag down once we're airborne.

Language Tip

비행기 이, 착륙 시 승무원이 승객에게 요청하는 표현

- Fasten your seat belt.
- Stow you tray table.
- Raise / Open your window blind.
- Move your seat back to the upright position.
- Stow your baggage in the overhead bin / compartment or under the seat in front of you.

Conversation 4 In The Cabin

Flight attendant	Here's the menu, sir.
Passenger	Oh, thank you. By the way, how long is the flight?
Flight attendant	Eleven hours.
Passenger	But captain said we arrived at 14:45.
Flight attendant	That's local time.
Passenger	Oh, of course.
Flight attendant	Anything else I can do for you?
Passenger	No thanks, I'm fine.

Conversation 5 Meal Service

Flight attendant	Would you like beef or chicken, sir? Or the vegetarian option, the lasagne?
Passenger	Beef, please.
Flight attendant	Here we are. What would you like to drink?
Passenger	A glass of red wine, please.
Flight attendant	OK.
Passenger	Is it French?
Flight attendant	No, it's South African wine. It's very nice. Would you like to try it?
Passenger	Yes, thank you.
Flight attendant	Enjoy your meal.

Conversation 6 Handling Complaints

Flight attendant	Hello, can I help you?
Passenger	Yes, I ordered a special meal online, but it hasn't arrived yet.
Flight attendant	Okay, I can go and check. Which meal did you order?
Passenger	The gluten free option.
Flight attendant	Oh, I'm sorry. I think there has been a mistake. We just gave out the last gluten free meal.
Passenger	But I ordered it online!
Flight attendant	I'm so sorry, there must have been some confusion. You can have anything else from our menu.
Passenger	I can only eat gluten-free dishes, so that's no use. Also, my screen is not working!
Flight attendant	I'm very sorry about that, ma'am.
Passenger	It's twelve-hour flight! What am I supposed to do? No food and no TV.
Flight attendant	Ma'am, we can offer you an upgrade to business class, so that you have a working TV screen.
Passenger	Business class? Let's go!
Flight attendant	Follow me, please, ma'am.

Essential Phrases

Would it be alright if we put your bag in the overhead bin?
It' s standard procedure for (take-off), sir.
Anything else I can do for you?

What would you like to drink?
Would you like to try it?
I can go and check.

Essential Words

Overhead bin / compartment	Upright position
emergengy exit	Special meal
Window blind	Gluten-free
Seat back	Upgrade
Standard procedure	Business class

Answers

UNIT 1. Reservation

Page 13

Practice : Speaking

- Good morning, Reservations.
- Let me check. Yes, we have availability for January 5th.
- I can offer you our best rate of $140 per night.
- Im afraid that is room only.
- Could you please give me your name and credit card details?
- Thank you, Mr. Gardiner. Your reservation number is MH478PT. We look forward to seeing you in January. Goodbye.

Page 16

Practice : Speaking

- Good morning.
- Could you tell me your reservation number, please?
- Mr. Jackson on February twelfth?
- That' s fine. I' ve cancelled your reservation.
- No, there is no charge.
- Of course. Thank you for your call. Goodbye.

UNIT 2. Check-in

Page 26

Practice : 손님의 대답에 어울리는 인사말 넣기

- Good morning.
- How are you
- Nice

Page 29

Practice : Speaking

- Good afternoon. Welcome to our hotel.
- Could I have your credit card?
- Would you like a wake-up call?
- Good. 6 a.m. would you like a newspaper?
- Yes, that' s fine.
- Breakfast is between 7:00 and 10:30.

Page 32

Practice : I'm afraid so. / I'm afraid not.

1. I'm afraid the hotel doesn' t accept cheques.
2. I'm afraid we have no vacancies this evening.
3. I'm afraid you have to check out at noon.
4. I'm afraid that' s the best rate I can offer you, sir.
5. I'm afraid not.
6. I'm afraid so.
7. I'm afraid not.

Page 35

Practice : 빈 칸에 적당한 단어 고르기

1. store	2. suggest	3. quite	4. get
5. for	6. from	7. to	

Practice : Speaking

- Good morning. How can I help you?
- Ah, yes. Mr. Weiler.
- Our check in time is 2 pm, sir.
- You' re welcome to store your suitcase with us, sir.
- May I suggest you go for a cup of coffee in the coffee shop?
- Just go around the corner to your left, sir.

UNIT 3. Looking After Guests - Concierge

Page 43

Practice : 보기의 단어 중 빈 칸에 알맞은 단어 고르기

1. catch 2. turn 3. map 4. pleasure
5. circle

Practice : Speaking

- Good evening, ma'am. Can I help you?
- Let me give you a map of the city. The hotel is here. I'll circle it for you.
- The train station is about ten minutes' walk away.
- So turn right out of the hotel. Walk along Green Street and turn left onto Madison Avenue. The train station is on your right.
- You're welcome.

Page 46

Practice : 문장 연결하기

1. How can I help you?
2. What time do you need a taxi?
3. As soon as the fax arrives, we'll bring it to your room.
4. I'll order you a taxi for a quarter to ten.
5. I'll call your room when the taxi arrives.

Practice : Speaking

- Good morning, sir. Can I help you?
- I'm sorry, sir. I'm afraid the hotel doesn't have a swimming pool.
- I'm sorry, sir.

Page 47

Practice : Speaking

- Good morning, madam. How can I help you?
- Of course, madam. What time do you need the taxi?
- OK, madam. I'll call your room when your taxi arrives.
- You're welcome.

UNIT 4. Communication Problems – Front Desk

Page 53

Practice : 맞는 형태의 동사 고르기

1. spell 2. repeat 3. catch 4. call
5. I'll put 6. read

Practice : Speaking

- Good morning. Metro Hotel. How can I help you?
- I'm sorry. I didn't quite catch that. Would you mind repeating your name?
- I'm sorry. I still can't understand. Could you possibly call back?
- That's much better, madam. One moment I'll put you through to the restaurant.

UNIT 5. At Breakfast and The Bar

Page 59

Practice : Speaking

- Good morning, madam.
- Could I have your room number, please?
- Are you going to have the continental breakfast or something from the menu?
- Here's the menu if you'd like to order something from the kitchen.
- Would you like tea or coffee?
- Would you like milk or lemon?
- And can I bring you some toast?
- Of course, madam. Feel free to help yourself to the buffet.
- Here's your tea, madam. Enjoy your breakfast.

Page 63

Practice – 자연스러운 대화가 될 수 있도록 문장의 순서 쓰기

5-1-2-8-4-6-7-3-9

Practice : Speaking

- Good evening, sir.
- I' m fine, thank you. What can I get you?
- We have Grolsch, Heineken and Budweiser.
- Well, Grolsch is very popular.
- Here you are, sir.
- That' ll be four pounds.
- Of course, sir. Could you give me your room number, please?
- Thank you, sir. Could you sign here, please?

Page 66

Practice : 빈 칸에 들어갈 전치사 고르기

1. with 2. to 3. at 4. to
5. on

UNIT 6. In The Restaurant

Page 75

Practice : 예의바르게 말하기

1. May I take your coat?
2. Good evening. Welcome to the restaurant.
3. Let me give you a menu.
4. Are you having wine this evening?
5. Le me know when you' re ready to order.

Page 77

Practice – 자연스러운 대화가 될 수 있도록 문장의 순서 쓰기

1-5-9-2-6-3-8-4-7-10

Page 79

Practice : 보기의 단어 중 빈 칸에 알맞은 단어를 골라 넣기

1. May 2. Was 3. by 4. afraid
5. accept 6. use 7. enter 8. press

UNIT 7. **Housekeeping / Room Service / Laundry Service**

Page 86

Practice : bring / take 연습

1. take 2. bring 3. take 4. bring

Practice : 문장 연결하기

1. B 2. A 3. D 4. E 5. F 6. C

Page 88

Practice : Speaking

- Good evening. Room Service [name] speaking. How can I help you?
- No, it isn' t too late. What would you like?
- Of course. What kind of beer would you like?
- Would you like ketchup with your burger?
- It' ll be with you in 15 minutes.

UNIT 8. **Guest Services**

Page 99

Practice : 문장에 알맞은 전치사 골라 넣기

1. up 2. on 3. at 4. for
5. in 6. of 7. of

Page 105

Practice : 비교급 만들기

1. bigger 2. cheaper 3. more expensive
4. more popular 5. smaller 6. closer

UNIT 9. Check-Out

Page 112

Practice : 주어진 단어를 이용해 문장 만들기

1. Could you sign here, please?
2. How was your stay?
3. Did you have anything from the minibar?
4. Have a safe trip home.
5. Are you using the same credit card?

Page 113

Practice : Speaking

- Of course, sir. What was your room number?
- Please have a look at this printout, sir.
- Could I have your credit card, sir?
- Could you sign here, please?
- Certainly, sir. Here you are.
- You' re welcome. Did you enjoy your stay?
- We hope to see you again, sir. Have a safe trip.

Page 117

Practice : 보기의 단어 중 빈 칸에 들어갈 알맞은 단어 고르기

1. remove 2. pass 3. happen 4. put
5. hear 6. Adjust

Page 118

Practice : 주어진 문장을 'look forward to 동사-ing'를 사용하여 정중한 표현으로 바꾸기

1. I look forward to seeing you again soon.
2. I look forward to welcoming you back to the Metro Hotel.
3. I look forward to showing you our new gym and swimming pool.
4. I look forward to hearing your thoughts on the new hotel design.
5. I look forward to reading your comments in our visitors book.

UNIT 11. **In The Cabin**

Page 139

Practice : 빈 칸에 정중하게 사과하는 표현 넣기

- I'm sorry
- I do apologize.
- I assure you it won't happen again.
- That's all right.

저자소개

■ 명수진(SOO JIN, MYUNG)

- 프랑스 AGROSUP, DIJON Mastère Professionnel(Bac +6), 와인 경영학 (Connaissance et Commerce Internationale du Vin) 전공
- (주) 아시아나항공 캐빈 승무원
- SKT Leaders Club 인천공항 라운지 팀장
- Crystal Valley Country Club 기획.마케팅 지배인
- (주)동아원, Vin.ga 지배인
- 서비스 컨설턴트

현) 광운대학교 정보과학교육원 관광경영학부 강사

■ 류기환(KI HWAN, RYU)

- 경희대학교 경영대학원 관광경영학과(관광경영전공) / 경영학 석사
- 경희대학교 정경대학원 무역학과(국제경영전공) / 경영학 박사
- 세계여행신문사 대표이사 겸 발행인
- 크루즈씨씨케이 대표이사

현) 광운대학교 스마트융합대학원 관광산업전공 주임교수
광운대학교 정보과학교육원 관광경영학부 교수
의정부시 행정혁신위원(교육문화분과)
한기범 희망재단 기획홍보이사
MBC ECONOMY 편집위원
국제관광무역학회 회장

Essential English for Hotel and Hospitality Professionals

호텔 & 관광업무 필수 실용 영어

2020년 3월 2일 초 판 발행
2023년 9월 10일 1판 2쇄 발행

저 자 명수진 · 류기환

발행인 한 인 환
발행처 도서출판 **기 문 사**
등 록 1978. 8. 9. NO. 6-0637
주 소 서울시 동대문구 안암로 50-1(용두동) 홍신빌딩 3층
전 화 02) 2265-7214 / 922-8662~8663
팩 스 02) 922-8772

homepage : www.kimoonsa.co.kr
e-mail : book@kimoonsa.co.kr

ISBN : 978-89-7723-856-5 93740

저자와의 협의하에 인지생략

정가 : 10,000원